FORMS FROM CHAOS

"I will pour chaos into fourteen lines"
Edna St Vincent Millay (c 1945)

With Love

Ian Ehr~~~

March 2024

Also by Ian Enters

Poetry
>Outside this Communion (Outposts 1977)
>Calendar of the Greeks (Outposts 1981)
>Build and Break (Envoi 1991)
>5 Artists (Snig Hill Gallery 2013)
>Word Hoard (Macadie Books/Amazon 2020)

Novels
>Shadow (Weidenfeld & Nicolson 1989)
>Up to Scratch (Weidenfeld & Nicolson 1990)
>Redhead (Macadie Books/Amazon 2020)

FORMS FROM CHAOS

Sonnets and Other Poems

Ian Enters

T

Troubador Publishing Ltd
Unit E2 Airfield Business Park,
Harrison Road, Market Harborough,
Leicestershire. LE16 7UL
Tel: 0116 2792299
Email: books@troubador.co.uk
Web: www.troubador.co.uk

ISBN 978 1805143 017

British Library Cataloguing in Publication Data.
A catalogue record for this book is available from the British Library.

Printed and bound in Great Britain by 4edge Limited
Typeset in 10pt Minion Pro by Troubador Publishing Ltd, Leicester, UK

For my family and my friends
and in memory of my brother, Gary.

Contents

In truth the prison into which we doom
Ourselves, no prison is; and hence for me,
In sundry moods, 'twas pastime to be bound
Within the Sonnet's scanty plot of ground.

William Wordsworth (c 1807 from his sonnet 'Nuns Fret Not')

Introduction and Brief History of the Sonnet in English Literature

Over the last few years my poetry writing has tended towards more traditional forms and this book celebrates that experience. The primary spur towards publication was the enforced self-isolation caused by government imposed restrictions during the Covid pandemic. Inward-looking and renewal through reading, closeness to the immediate environment and solitary walking within a repeated structure for every day created a fragile self-sufficiency and focus on a daily task – the writing of a sonnet as a discipline and a reassurance that my mind was not atrophying with increasing age and lack of stimulus.

My earlier poetic practice mainly found expression in what is often called "free verse", in which meaning and development within a sequence of thoughts finds its own instinctive structures both from line to line and section to section. There is great satisfaction in honing that process to create a tight and rich outcome appropriate for its subject matter and moving to a resolution. Perhaps this is the purpose of all creation, not just poetry. I wanted to find and speak with "my own voice" rather than as a derivative from others' practice. Of course, such an intention is impossible to achieve and there are echoes throughout a poet's work of others' influences and ways of being, but I relish the challenge of writing with integrity and from my own personality whether within free or formal structures.

It is tempting to adduce the main reason for this book is that with age I have become less experimental in my writing, more clad in the clothes of the past, and there may be some truth in that. I have studied the canon of literature throughout my life and revelled in its variety within evolving forms. This absorption brings wonderful enjoyment of the brilliance of poets balanced on the edge and finding new routes into visionary expression. It is the poets of visionary power who capture my heart as well as my head from all sorts of backgrounds, cultures and times. In fact I would argue that all fine poets must create visions into the heart of existence. The ways into such a frisson, when truth is recognised and felt to be true, encompass all language available to the poet from rhyming couplets to Petrarchan sonnets to free verse, rapping, prose poems, and ways of writing yet to be created for a particular purpose. My poetry reading during self-isolation explored a wide range of work, but my own writing found its main focus in the rhymes, the rhythms and the power of the stressed line. The repeated structure of the sonnets with their minor adjustments when they worked, and false notes when they didn't, reflected the day by day routines I followed.

Another possible reason why I have found myself working within either the Petrarchan or Elizabethan sonnet more often is the sheer pleasure of returning to structured word-play and finding that meaning evolves from the form as much as from the initial intention to explore a particular theme or subject. By plotting a rhyme sequence of fairly haphazard words and then creating bridges between them I have managed to surprise myself with refreshed vocabulary, images and linkages. Writers can inhabit a repetitive range of vocabulary and sentence structure and, by looking through my extensive output over many years, it is clear that, despite my best efforts, the same words and phrases do recur. There is an irony in the fact that choosing a set form in which to work released me from a personally created strait-jacket of which I had too little awareness. In addition, I greatly enjoyed pushing the boundaries, tweaking the form.

That may say something of the essential need for me to have a structure for living, but not an enforced conformity. Sometimes the occasional break, clunk, spondee and intrusion of anapaests disturbed the flow of the iambic pentameter and I welcomed this infusion of irregularity when it seemed to match the mood of the sonnet.

Finally, and perhaps most forceful in its application, I return to the issue of "individual creation" and that often stated compulsion that artists need to find "their own voice". When society is relatively stable, when affairs of state and the well-being of its people are reasonably wedded, when the horsemen of the apocalypse seem far away, then creators may feel free to express from their own individual circumstances and experience, to delve deeply into the immediate and conjure magic through ever more idiosyncratic ways of being and expressing. However, now, when the "centre can not hold" and chaos looms (perhaps chaos is ever looming), I feel the need to find some mutually recognised and communally accepted order in which to frame my words. Others might refuse such a route and bounce back images of chaos from the cracked mirror of our lives and the social conditions of the human world. Certainly the impact of war early in the twentieth century seemed to do so. I, however, have needed a self-imposed ordering to manage my own feelings. My reason for this book is as much a political statement of the need for social cohesion as are my personal reasons for using established forms of poetic expression. The sonnet often moves from the great ego of "I" to a sense of communal understanding and resolution. This work is a sharing of both a particular time for me and a shared experience for almost all of us.

Collections of sonnets were regarded as the pinnacle of performance by the poets of the Renaissance, and these poets were also linked to the classical tradition through the education of an upper-class who received intensive and rigorous classical and rhetorical training. The power of the Elizabethan sonnet rested in an increasingly personal and immediate style of alternate rhyming lines, couplets or less frequently the

Petrarchan quatrain. The subject matter normally expressed formal romantic yearnings and courtship. One of the most well known of Shakespeare's sonnets, but often not recognised as such in its context, appears in *Romeo and Juliet* when the star-struck masked lovers first meet at the ball. Here there are two voices in balance marrying love and faith into an exquisite tentative avowal. "If I profane with my unworthiest hand...." says Romeo asking for a kiss. "Palm to palm is holy palmer's kiss" replies Juliet. The sonnet ends with the fulfilment of prayer and a holy kiss is granted. Here is the Elizabethan sonnet in its purest form, but Shakespeare's collected published sonnets are much more personal, challenging, and rooted in exploration of time and relationships. Sydney, Surrey, Spenser, and Wyatt were also rooting their sonnets in more immediate and personal, but carefully disguised, subject matter. It could be dangerous to express certain emotional attachments or religious beliefs too clearly. The study of Elizabethan sonnets often becomes a study of riddles and conundrums, or a deliberate play on the form for an amusing effect – "My mistress when she walks, treads on the ground!" And for extended narrative, Edmund Spenser employed what is known as the Spenserian stanza in the Faerie Queene, an allegorical tale of chivalry and the battle between two sides of the same coin – Una (good Queen Elizabeth) and Duessa (sorceress masquerading as Una). There were layers upon layers to peel away when following the dangerous intricacies of court politics. It has ever been so.

It is sometimes ignored or forgotten, however, that the first sonnet sequence of any note was that by Anne Locke published in 1560. She predated Philip Sidney's sequence of *Astrophil and Stella*. Her *Meditations of a Penitent Sinner* uses what is known as the Elizabethan form and epitomizes the use of the sonnet for exploring religious themes and expiation through confession and prayer. Later, in the seventeenth century, John Donne's religious sonnets gave dramatic rebirth to this theme, but in a more public way. He spoke from the pulpit. Anne Locke spoke from her private heart. Lady Mary Wroth, at the end of the sixteenth century, published an extended sonnet sequence mainly about coping with depression. It received much acclaim. Ben Jonson enjoyed it, but the subject matter may have chimed with his personal knowledge of the "black dog". Both Anne Locke and Lady Mary Wroth introduced a private voice into the sonnet with less formal and less conventional elements within the form.

It is rare for Milton to be described as clear and unambiguous, but his major sonnets mark a shift into direct expression of a personal state. He shrugs away the trammels of classical subject matter and cultural expectations and, without the metaphorical allusions and complexities of the metaphysical poets, he speaks his own voice:

> *When I consider how my light is spent*
> *Ere half my days in this dark world and wide*
> *And that one talent which is death to hide*
> *Lodged with me useless, ...*
> *"Doth God exact day-labour, light denied?"*

There is no hiding place, no hidden corner, but a bald powerful statement of a personal plight. He is within and of the Reformation and just as Luther could agonise over his bowel movements, and Churches could be stripped of their ostentation, so the Bible could be shared among all people and each person could read and speak themselves in supposed equality.

Aphra Behn, product of the Restoration in the seventeenth century, dramatist and occasional poet, whisked away the dark privations of life with contemporary references, satirical observances and downright sexual enjoyment. Her only extant sonnet, however, deals with the death of a young child. *Epitaph on the Tombstone of a Child, the last of seven that died before* is a public message of support and consolation:

> *This little, silent, gloomy monument*
> *Contains all that was sweet and innocent...*

From this antithetical opening, Behn describes the translation of the child into glory greeted by angels and celebrated in song. It is a triumph of hope and consolation in a time of the libertines.

When Coleridge and Wordsworth produced the Lyrical Ballads in the 1790s, thus kick-starting what is known as the Romantic movement, they asserted the need for poetry to speak about and for "ordinary" people. I have never been at ease with that terms "ordinary" or "common". Such adjectives embed a class system destructive of inclusion and shared respect. Coleridge, Wordsworth, and Southey were not of peasant stock! They attended Oxford or Cambridge from what might be called middle or upper class backgrounds, but they did challenge the prevailing style of heroic couplet classical satirical verse, and incurred the wrath of the critics. The French Revolution across the channel and the deep-seated fear that such dangerous thought could reach England galvanised a back-lash. It was a betrayal of the ruling classes by the very people of the higher classes which seemed so dangerous. Shelley was a prime example of this betrayal and his subject matter in *Queen Mab, Prometheus Unbound*, the *Cenci*, and, of course, *The Mask of Anarchy*, made him "persona non grata" in England, nor could most of his work be published until after his death. This minor aristocrat must have been virtually the only one to be denied custody of his children by the courts – a lucky escape for both of the children, but not for his young deserted wife, Harriet, who committed suicide. Shelley's sonnet, *Ozymandias*, may have been first written as part of what we might call writing workshops held with Leigh Hunt, who supported the later romantic poets. David Fairer, retired professor of English Literature and fine historical fiction novelist of the 18th century, introduced me to Leigh Hunt's sonnet, *On a Lock of Milton's Hair*. It is a most glorious Petrarchan sonnet. Its delicate and loving observation of a small strand of hair develops into a powerful celebration of "affectionate eternity".

The regular task was to write a sonnet within twenty minutes. My best shot has been twenty five minutes, but much revision is always necessary and even then the waste bin beckons. These sonnets and the Petrarchan style odes of John Keats mark a continuity from Coleridge's seminal instinctive connection to seen and unseen natural powers working on human lives, and Wordsworth's deep and personal development of Nature's reach into intimations of immortality from childhood onwards. But, once again, as with Anne Locke, it was a female sonneteer, Charlotte Turner Smith, who predated and informed the Romantic movement. Gothic writing was becoming the vogue and that capacity for wildness and freedom of spirit speaks through Smith's work. *Sonnet on being Cautioned about Walking on a Headland* from her collection *Elegiac Sonnets* shows this theme well:

> *Is there a solitary wretch who hies*
> *To the tall cliff, with starting pace or slow,*
> *And, measuring, views with wild and hollow eyes*
> *Its distance from the waves that chide below …*

Shelley's first published work before going to Oxford was his Gothic writing. Arguably Charlotte Smith's influential work was one of the many stimuli for Mary Shelley to create *Frankenstein*. Smith certainly prefigured the re-awakening of the English sonnet to encompass the unknown, the search for understanding in Nature and the freedom to do so.

The sonnets of the Romantic movement are often observations of a specific scene or situation with a natural or classical context and the personal reflections and conclusions that the poet derives from that observation. The decayed statue of the great king *Ozymandias* in the desert becomes Shelley's symbol for the vanity of man's self-importance and power in the grasp of Nature and time. Wordsworth's *View from Westminster Bridge* becomes a call for people to be open to the touching power and beauty of this scene and not to "pass by in dullness". Keats's *On First Reading Chapman's Homer* speaks of how imagination extends vision into realms far beyond immediate experience and transfixes the spiritual heart. But, with the recognition of supposedly "ordinary" voices, the peasant poet became the five minute stars of the moment to be picked up, celebrated and discarded. Foremost among these were Blake, Clare, Burns, Thompson. Clare's "I Am" is not a sonnet, but its two six line stanzas have a sonnet's exquisite endeavour to describe and come to some sort of terms with his circumstances. The use of "I Am" harks back to God's words to Moses from the burning bush, is echoed in Coleridge's words in Biographia Literaria where he sees himself within and at one with the creation of God, but Clare in his asylum flings this back with the lonely desperation of the lost and deserted:

I am the self-consumer of my woes.

There were many others, particularly women, whose voices have hardly been heard, although recent research has brought to the fore excellent female poets in every genre – *British Women Poets of the Long Eighteenth Century* edited by Paula R. Backscheider and Catherine E. Ingrassia provides a formidable list with examples.

Victorian society with its patriarchal world under the aegis of a matriarch brought recognition for more female voices into the field of sonnets. Elizabeth Barrett Browning is justly famous for her sonnets of love. *Sonnets from the Portuguese* were written after her elopement with Robert Browning. They are not translated from Portuguese. Portuguese was Robert Browning's nickname for Elizabeth – don't know why! Her sonnet *Grief* probably deals with the death of her brother Edward in a sailing accident. Christina Rossetti took up the mantle of sonneteer. Her most famous sonnet *Remember* is often used at funerals. The purpose of a sonnet had become again a formal recognition of personal and shared feeling in the work of the Victorian women poets. It is worth noting that Elizabeth Barrett Browning came a very close second to winning the poet laureate mantle, but Tennyson received it. He was the queen's firm favourite and

Tennyson's *In Memoriam* her consolation for the loss of Albert. After Elizabeth's death at the age of 55, Robert Browning's work became the more celebrated achievement and the preferred literary form for a successful writer was fast becoming the novel or a narrative conversation.

The sonnet remained an essential part of a poet's armoury as an occasional poem, but the first world war heralded increasing experimentation from poets trying to speak of appalling and desperate scenes. The cosy world of *The Old Village Grantchester* by Rupert Brooke with its neat rhymes and "Is there honey still for tea?" was smashed in the trenches from where the voices of poets spoke for the thousands of victims with a "terrible beauty". Brooke's war sonnets are all pre-war in sentiment and still used as symbols of the nation by so-called patriots. They do not express the reality of experience. "If I should die, think only this of me..." Other poets demanded much wider thoughts and awareness than "A corner of a foreign field that is for ever England." Blunden put to one side his early pastoral poetry. Kipling found the voice of soldiers in his Barrack Room Ballads, but his early jingoism became a pustulating sore in his heart with the death of his son. It was with W.H. Auden that the sonnet returned to speak truth to power. His *Sonnets from China* are condemnations of war and its terrible results. I find 'Here War is Simple' the most telling of them. The first eight lines in two four line verses are in formal pentameters with a regular rhyme scheme. The first four lines describe daily lives of apparently ordinary actions- telephone call, milk being drunk, a map. They are simple but increasingly infused with the extraordinary. The telephone talks to the receiver of the call. A map is marked with troop movements. The next four lines express the growing fear behind the attempt to keep doing the ordinary as people die. The volta- the final six lines- becomes ever more terse, stripped of all but the essential, as if Auden's own control is close to breaking under the weight of the terrifying consequences of lies and propaganda. Using more words for such evil is unnecessary, impossible. Ideas may or may not have truth within them, but the two names on the map are reality. The first name conjures the massacre of at least three hundred thousand Chinese and the second of the murder of many many thousands in a German Concentration Camp. The last vestige of the poet's control remains in a three line repeated pattern and hammer blow of single syllable rhymes: *'die' 'lie' 'now' 'Nanking. Dachau.'* And so human destruction of other humans continues in every generation and our desire for peace sometimes appears a futile aspiration even as the planet on which we live demands our united care for our continued existence. Is it time for prayer?

Some days, although we cannot pray, a prayer
utters itself. So, a woman will lift
her head from the sieve of her hands and stare
at the minims sung by a tree, a sudden gift.

This is the opening quatrain from Carol Ann Duffy's sonnet, *Prayer*. It is a touching and beautifully poised poem and almost brings Anne Locke's sixteenth century meditative voice into the present, but Duffy's conclusion has the reassuring daily cadence of the shipping forecast as its concluding and surprising prayer: "Rockall, Malin, Dogger, Finisterre." Prayers find themselves in every connection, every experience. Sonnets, whatever their subject matter, articulate prayerful moments in a studied way.

So, at the risk of invidious comparisons and raised eyebrows at my hubris in presenting this collection, here are sixty one poems, mainly sonnets interlaced with a number of other forms regular and irregular. Perhaps one or two will appeal and even strike a kindred's chord of recognition, but I pray for your indulgence when my raw attempts fail the test of eighteenth century fluidity and control of the iambic pentameter. Chaos does threaten even as I battle for an assured verse form.

DAY BY DAY

Spotting Stars

*four stresses and mixture of couplets and quatrains – sixteen lines
in two stanzas.*

These walls have eyes but they are blind
To where my clapping palms bring hope
To bleach the virus with soft soap.
Do we save mankind by being kind?
Too many years have cradled blight
And chapped my hands now split and sore
Until decay has reached the core
Where, in this cell, I take my flight.

Zoom a camera at my head.
My beard is white. My eyes hold dread
Lest this confinement is a trap
Within a maze without a map.
A prisoner must learn to cope,
To throw aside his moping rope
And spot the stars where he may find
The lights to magnify his mind.

Dust

four stresses and mixture of couplets and quatrains – sixteen lines in two stanzas

Hold to my heart. Stay safe and strong.
Interrogating power does not mean
I boggle at a never-ending screen.
Better seek a cheerful thoughtful song.
Film, books, shared stories can amuse.
I feel no guilt in armchair cosy snooze.
It takes an age of living to adjust
And not rekindle a forgotten lust.

The drive is on to trim off fat to lean,
To vacuum the house to pristine clean.
This is my patch where I alone belong.
It shows my sluggish life and so I long
To bring my mind and body to a fuse
Of action, but yet I have to choose
To be behind these walls where yes I must
Remind myself I am but dust and dust.

Large Thoughts

Petrarchan

No journeys, I travel where I'm able
From door to door and at each entry bless
My safety, my dog, my steadiness.
Alone I am alive and do what's viable.
Social media messages seem to care.
I read advice wherein I may decide
Small actions to help the hours divide
Large thoughts while seated in this chair.

I wash my hands to slough away disease.
I ponder whether Wednesday is the date
For an April Fool. Is there is a fate
Written by a God who loves to tease?
My dog ambles to my feet and sighs.
He knows his walk is later. Down he lies.

2nd April 2020 Birthday

Petrarchan

My younger brother, dead, it is his day
And him ungraved as yet and I still
Unquiet with what is left, no will
To leave, no will to help him stay.
Six Brownie snaps of family black and white
With him, the smallest, gurgling, playful child,
While sisters, brothers, watch the birdie, smile
And Mother holds him full of hopeful light.

Then what's to come was shrouded in the night.
Father's heart stops and Mother's too.
Adult children do what they must do.
And brother, dead, paints away, his sight
Undimmed by drugs and mind's decay.
Now smile for his release, his time to play.

Schism

Petrarchan

If, in time, I'm asked the way she walked
And how she faced the world with fearless eyes
To help, to challenge, to banish lies,
I'd smile, opaquely neutral, for we talked
In riddles which only we could know.
Our secrets hid our secrets to keep or share
In a lip-twitch or an eye's sudden flare
Like the light before the birthday-candle-blow.

I knew love faltered and died when her eye
Grew dark as midnight under a thunder-cloud.
She pursed her mouth and never spoke aloud
A flimsy thought. Such speech would be a lie.
What made this schism in her heart for me?
The chain I locked on her. I kept the key.

Puppy Training

Petrarchan

Another quiet day for dog and me.
We snooze, we talk, we manufacture facts
Inside this house where memory triggers acts.
Another training treat? A cup of tea?
"Find!" I call. He searches, finds to crunch
A tasty treat by which he learns a word.
"Good dog!" I praise him. Is it so absurd
To school a pup with praises and a munch?

But on the radio "Stay at home" is said
A three word slogan, "Getting Brexit done."
Another order? "Austerity is fun!"
A propagandist's slogan builds on dread.
Less income tax for rich, less pay for me.
Servitude is loyalty. Of course I'm free.

Freely Given Silence

Mainly Elizabethan

My inward voice is hesitant with doubt.
My outward voice rings trumpet truth so clear
That if my secret heart became a shout
Would I lose myself or lose my hidden fear?
But trust in others to respect my pain
Requires a courage to confront the test
Of finding words to break the fettering chain
And free the knowing locked inside my chest.

I would be whole without such vain conceit
That there is worth in delving for the meat
Of meaning when silence is a finer prize
Than building stories mingling truth with lies.
Such freely given silence is my gain
So I remain in silence to stay sane.

NOW

Petrarchan with shortened Volta

NOW applauds its precious hold-me moment.
It tells the time, the second I'm alive,
But if I stumble, lift me, help me strive
To find NOW's solace when I would lament
My loss of freedom behind and still ahead.
Down through the rings of Dante's abyss
I fall with old burdens and will not miss
Stalagmites of ice. They are ghosts of the dead,
Who taint what might be with a Judas kiss.

Oh lift me to the heavens in rainbow joys.
WAS and MIGHT BE are tiresome worn-out toys.
Just give me strength to dive sleek as a knife
Between the past and future of my life.

Top Down

Elizabethan

May I share a tale? It is no trouble
To speak of small concerns from each to each,
To sift the precious from the load of rubble
Until a path is found beyond the beach
Which brought me to this sad divided state.
I am high on Beachy Head, a sheer cliff,
Below a midget tanker with its freight
And on the shore a corpse already stiff.

I must confess it was a sad mistake
To think self-murder can become a cure.
I could have chosen tangled trees or lake
To hide from what I could no more endure.
But life is now beyond a pastor's reach.
I am the doleful corpse upon the beach.

Self-pity

Petrarchan/Elizabethan mixture

The fruit bowl holds a solitary apple,
Bronzed russet glowing from the embered fire.
Its Autumn colours speak of lost desire
Now I am one when once we were a couple.
A dram of golden whisky in the tumbler,
A splash of water for a piquant taste,
A deck of cards – let fortune be the number
When shuffled patience marks the time as waste.

The walls inside my mind are now much stronger.
They ward off sorrow with a heartfelt prayer
Consistent with the need to love and care
For those who will live on when I no longer
Munch the apple and sip the single malt.
Self-pity is a maudlin futile fault.

Dancing

Mainly Elizabethan but with half rhymes and arhythmic stresses

Toe-taps the rhythm of intensity.
White-stick clips black railings and is deaf
To all but staccato on the paving
And heaving of the chest at every breath.
Diaghelev designed the dance for Nureyev.
Astaire and Rogers twinkled it in style.
The longest conga reached a mighty mile
And here I am, blind and deaf, with two left

Feet crisping out a pattern on black ice.
So launch yourself, you creaking man, to catch
The dead end of this narrow cul-de-sac
For dancing is throwing bones as dice.
Bill Bailey showed us how to beat the clock.
Whoops! Another fall! It's cruel to mock.

Jig Not a Dirge

Petrarchan with rhyming couplets Volta

I woke, checked heart and limbs, more chipper
Than a sailor's breeze in a dawning sun
Hearing the hiss of waves, the starter's gun
To launch me from the harbour in a clipper.
I woke. Around me stood my family,
My friends, my people of now and the past.
Theirs is the sunshine. United they last
Shining and smiling, hugging happily.

No shadow can shroud this vision of joy.
The old man grins at his previous boy.
The wedding march christens a baby's head.
Jig not a dirge awakens the dead.
The sails belly out and we fly to sea.
Horizon gleams gold and our ship sails free.

Humours

Rhyming couplets

Three in the morning analysis breeds
Reversion to the humours, potent seeds
Of medical knowledge when our blood
And faeces teetered between drought and flood.
Sanguine, I shrug and huddle in bed
Until choler chokes me with its sudden dread.
I sit bolt upright, hair a hedgehog's quills,
Seized with images of convulsive ills.

Light has sunk into the oozings of night.
Melancholy inks my veins with its blight
Of despair. If death came now, who would care?
The cycle of life climbs an Escher's stair.
Through the blinds the first milky haze of day.
I cough green phlegm to continue the play.

Overthinking

Mainly rhyming couplets

Person of reason lurches into view,
Legs are twisted, torso and arms askew,
Tortured head is crowned with a dunce's cap
Bearing the legend "Neither seer nor sap".
Sere are the leaves from the Autumn tree.
Still squeezes sap from the harvest apple.
Unreason argues that limbs stay supple
If worked every day indefinitely.

But blind is the seer believing that
Time can be caught in a cider vat.
And wet is the sap judging that life
Is moulded clay at the end of a knife.
So temper reason with wisdom's art.
Too much thinking injures the heart.

Never Stop

Mainly Petrarchan

No. The last sonnet is devious and trite.
Last night at three before dawning I dreamed
Glistening silver fish gathered and teemed
Into Plato's cave with a message of light.
Today, despite sunshine on glittering frost,
Despite wondering if reason is lost
When instinct suggests a comfortable way
To reach resolution, I smile and say,

"Never stop searching. Always strive on the quest
To ponder the imponderable reach
Of a universe found on a pebble beach.
Even as brain and body shriek "Rest!"
Refuse the temptation of quiet belief
Which adverts assert brings instant relief.

Artificial Intelligence

Petrarchan

Cogito ergo sum. I think. I am.
A simple truth to measure I might think
But layered meanings lurk beyond the brink
Of this dark lake above the beavers' dam.
In metaphors more truthfulness is found
Than in stark memories of what and when,
A trivial pursuit, a disregard for Zen.
Robots, plotting step on step, are bound
To linear progression and the link
Of retrieval systems clunking into play.
It thinks. It is. But does it live to say
Its spirit is of sunshine through a chink?
I fear to think "I am" has now become
Redundant and AI is number one.

Choice

Petrarchan

"Choose one of these three sticks to carry back."
The first is straw-yellow, smooth with a crown
Like a hip-bone ball or a dome of brown
Pitted by dog-chasing on this frozen track.
The second is lumpish greened with stiff moss,
Forked at one end and weighted the other
With a block like a brick. It lands with a pother
On ice-filmed puddles. Leave it there. No loss.

Ah, here is the third. It is straight not too long.
It's black and silver – a conjuror's stick.
No nodules, no warping, no party trick
For a Scottie dog to clench in his strong
Jaws all the way from park to the front door.
"Drop! Leave it there. Tomorrow there'll be more."

Inheritance

Mainly Petrarchan

I make an island space beside a pile
Of papers, books, magazines, torn apart
Envelopes. Elbow nudges a corner file.
In my hands your parcel. Where to start?
More cellotape than card. Scissors snip
To the heart. I know what you have sent
And wish you had kept it back in Kent,
Not paid first class postage for this trip.

A cliché: here it is heavy as lead
In Victorian binding. My Mother
Would want me to have it with no other
Left to inherit but she is long dead.
I open the frontispiece for the family verse.
The last name is mine. A blessing or a curse?

Wet Sand

*Almost a thousand thousand years ago a family walked along
a beach at Happisburgh in Norfolk, England. Their fossilized
footprints remained intact and visible until about ten years ago
when stormy seas took them into oblivion.*

Petrarchan

My dog and I print water-marks in sand
By the tainted yellow foam from a timid sea.
We plant each step as an anomaly:
Neither in ocean nor firm-footing on land.
The dog laps salt, shakes silver from his coat,
Then scoots across the mirror with his man.
In a moment the trace of where we ran
Is lost. He pants, thirst gravelling his throat.

A mile from here a family traced its walk,
Feet bare, in line, crab-hunting among rocks.
Their passing did not vanish. Their printing mocks
The shadows where I write and sometimes talk
As if a thousand thousand years were in my hand
To cast a lasting message in wet sand.

For Tim Brooke-Taylor

Villanelle

When death must come, for it must come one day,
Let it be joyous in its grasp on me
From dark to light so goes the old man's play.

A smile, a greeting, let me no longer stay
To balance living in a cage or free
When death must come, for it must come one day.

From dark to light so goes the old man's play.
Water my runners. They will taste of me.
I'll till the ground enriching it with clay.

I'll cast my clouts when blossom heralds May
And hold embraces warmly happily
When death does come. It has to come one day.

From dark to light so goes the old man's play
And Tim Brooke-Taylor modelled this for me
When death must come, for it must come one day.

Goodies will find the absurdest things to say
And greet news-bringers with sidelong winks and glee
When death must come, for it must come one day
From dark to light so goes the old man's play.

Spit and Polish

aa/bb/a – loose rhyming five line stanzas

Each unshaven Sunday, after butterfly cakes and tea,
He marches to the kitchen, keeping it Mother free
For serious business. The broadsheet daily or,
Less useful, tabloid is unfolded from the store
And smoothed across the table carefully.

He pulls a slatted tray from beneath the sink
And places it at right angles to his right, removes his links
And pops them in a pot beside the hot water tap.
He folds his baggy sleeves above the elbow, feels the nap
Of the cloth, then checks there's water in the kettle for his drink.

"Bring on the dancing girls!" He calls and in we come:
Five children bearing fourteen shoes, the weekly sum:
A pair for each, a black and brown for him, and Mother's
Blue and black for best, placed upon the paper cover
In size order. He pours a fingernail of water on a slug of rum.

With thin-bladed knife, he picks and scrapes the sludge,
Disappointed when a sole is clear of pickled mud,
And brushes all the dustings to a pan. He checks the heels
And roughened inners. He wonders if his older lad feels
That nail. He bangs it back. It'll do for another trudge

To catch the bus. He sups a snifter, checks the Kiwi tins
And places black and tanning brushes by their rims.
It's an old rag for the blue. He rummages in the tray
And finds it, smears baby shoes and Mother's day by day
Before the larger battle of the boot begins.

Laces are removed, examined for fraying and laid
Lengthways aglet to aglet. Scuffs are made
Whole before an equal brush of polish covers all.
Then working down the line, he buffs caps to balls
Of glass and leather uppers to an inlaid

Gloss. His elbow blurs and then he stops to spit
On a tiny mark. These boots are old and hardly fit
As they pass down the family, but they'll be clean
And gleaming. You'll not know where they've been
From looking. It's all that's left from doing army kit.

I used to imitate my father's concentrated frown,
Gather the household footwear from the hall, exclude
The Nike trainers, the slip-slops, plastic sandals
And brush the leather of blue, black and brown
To catch his face in each shining half a crown.

Note on Day by Day Poems

Many of these sonnets were written when I was living alone and in virtual isolation. They developed as a ritual daily exercise and were rarely triggered by an initial coherent idea. I often jotted down stream of consciousness rhyming words and these became triggers for different forms within and around the Petrarchan or Elizabethan sonnet. The first couple are not sonnets, but sixteen line poems in two verses with four stresses to each line in ballad form. As I became more used to the process, not necessarily better at it, I juggled and played with different line lengths and the use of the volta (the second section of a sonnet) became a more flexible instrument, but I still worked to bind lines into strong units of abba, abab or aabb. The process gave me a freedom to work within the established forms to release whatever was filling my mind at a specific time in my self-isolation cell.

This "Day by Day" section initially tends to deal with immediate matters – the sonnet as a small song. The topics cover small observations; routine activities; social media and relationships from afar; my puppy; rather too much in-dwelling. These are interspersed with more formal substance such as the sonnet about my younger brother's death; the impact of an imagined inheritance; a particular place; end of a relationship. I can see connections between some of the sonnets and I collected them initially in order of writing and discarded many. Now I have found that process too tight a constraint and the order is determined by my whims. It is for the reader to find their own connections or not, as the case may be.

The section concludes with a villanelle and then a poem in stanzas of five lines each. The former celebrates the life and laments the death of Tim Brook Taylor, the latter commemorates my father as he fulfilled an apparently mundane task and turned it into a ritual. Perhaps the force of a poem lies in how meaning becomes infused with power beyond itself through the way it is constructed and, if performed, delivered.

THINKERS AND POETS

Analytic and Sensory Philosophy

Just write! But of what and when and why
When analytic words inside a storm
Are virus-ridden by a devious worm
Until my Babel Tower falls from the sky?
Pulses in my brain must seek a way
To speak a picture, rudimentary shape,
Offering a world behind a conjuror's drape.
Does Rorschack's inkblot have so little to say?

Faith in sensation seeks a shared meaning.
Within that cloud above Golgotha Hill,
One spots a jackdaw, another Quixotes' mill,
And yet a third turns to the wind leaning.
Held in the welcome arms of the chasing sky
He is carried away, learns to sing and to fly.

Carl Jung considers the futility of words in the continuous presence of silence

Here I am sitting in silence, pipe clenched
In my jaw, watching a thin white strand
Flicker as a smoke signal from raised land.
Is it an archetypal symbol wrenched
From Promethean past by lightning bolts and fires
Known through shared instinct beyond our verbal reach?
I rest in my apron, but yet I try to teach
That, when still from doing, words are still liars.

Solitude is my cherished fount of healing
And talk for me a torment of false branding.
Its thoughtless words make walls to understanding.
They kill connection to sharing human feeling.
May days of silence recover my wounded heart
When dagger words try to split me apart.

Cartier Bresson photograph on Pont des Arts

Sartre existed. On that bridge he stood
In Paris when the war was done and misted
Memories made nostalgia from bad and good
Events. He saw no trees inside the wood
And the wood itself was bombed into a smog.
This is the fact. All facts are fiction now
As is his scarf, coat, his quizzical brow.
Paris beyond is insubstantial fog.

An architect proffers a folder of designs
To build reality from steel and stone.
Pont des Arts shivers and makes moan,
Seine's estuarine mud scoured by mournful lines.
The words which sprang from fire are melted snow.
Nothing exists unless thinking makes it so.

Iris Murdoch – Metaphor for Morality and Mind's Mortality

Flower of wisdom, you open to the sun
Your gold and blue where the worker bee flew
To gather nectar, to build a comb so true
Your name became the worth your work had won –
A vision for the sovereignty of good.
But petals wilt and lose their holy power.
An image of worth becomes a poisonous flower.
Morality's metaphor is tangled in a wood.

How can a mind so active and alive
Lose its freshness in a year of slow days
And, as it dies, what are the secret ways
By which it may find peace and, at last, arrive
Where thought and conscious living is no more?
Her unselved gifts are left in rebirth's store

Kant – politics and aesthetics

Those self important words spoke just of you,
So I turned off the radio of Wild Western history.
Perhaps it was the lecture. It denied all mystery
And its teacherly mode asserted it's true
That black hats are bad lots and white hats are heroes.
The Chinese believe it's ever the reverse
For white means death – can mark a coming curse –
Colour coded bar of albino crows?

A fascist makes a propaganda play
To entertain and hide a power grab.
I sculpt my art to hone a raven's stab
To find the heart within a wall of clay.
When Kings use art to bluff and blind for gain,
My art expresses truth despite the pain.

Nietzche towards end of life beyond good and evil

He is only thirty eight but unaccountable
For actions fired from Superman's quick brain.
His wire-framed lenses hide lights which are insane
With futile fumbling for the mere impossible.
Words matter and are matter in themselves.
Prometheus gained their fire as maddened Pan
Spits in the face of God the sperm of man.
He brands self righteous books on bulging shelves.

When God is dead then man becomes as God
Strengthened by pain to rise again and fight
For the power to flood the world with neon light.
Free will? Frustrated will takes up the rod of God
To burn the stars or crumble into dust.
What's left? Moustache and syphilitic rust.

Lady Ottoline-Morrell's photo of nine friends at Garsington Manor with Bertrand Russell as main focus on the bottom step

Russell criticised involvement in World War 1 and was detained by the state briefly in 1918.

What's truth? He asked, buttocks on stony steps,
A central figure at Garsington's front door,
Slight and puckish. What life did he adore?
Ottoline's promiscuous notions or the sex?
She took the photo, popped her trophy there
With painter, dog and daughter at her side.
Tall notable men loom behind. Had she lied,
With his place down there while she pretended to care?

Truth and belief are entwined and allied
When death in trenches or dealt from the sky
Proffers white feathers to stifle the cry
In Conscience Cottage where his ideal died.
There's a lie in belief when logic is lost.
Truth's knowledge believes whatever the cost.

Photo-booth portrait of Ludwig Wittgenstein 1930 and Portrait for the Conferment of Scholarship Trinity College, Cambridge, 1926

"Statements are meaningful if they can be pictured."

When his eyes flinch sideways before the flash
Does he picture a similar curtain and booth,
With another man, eyes front, seeking to sooth
Yet another, flinching, whose thoughts are too rash
As he launches an assault on words to picture
What he had deduced as vital evidence
That imagined sepia is the extruded essence
Of fugitive truth? It will not endure.

Receipt of language knows no a priori rules.
He patterns it with echoes in the dark.
He wears this shabby jacket as a lark
Finding reality is but a quest for fools.
And what this image shows, you must allow,
Is metaphysical teasing then and now.

W H Auden and the ashes of anxiety

He chain-smokes cigarettes and they are kissed
By lip-puffs launching acrid clouds which wreath
Around his cratered face in a thought-filled mist.
Peaceful contemplation? But his eyes they seethe.
A fingernail plucks tobacco from between
Ochre teeth while he adds a tight and fervent line
To the ash-scattered paper. The queue he's seen
Holds displaced people fleeing the fascist sign.

His lover breaks. Law claims his love is crime.
Children are rickets-buckled and youth consumptive,
Yet the richly-decked are dancing in frantic time.
Their tears are dew-drop pearls trapped in a sieve.
Each fissure on his face maps out his pain.
Each inhalation kills to keep him sane.

Coleridge – offers a rock in the torrent of his talking

If talk could save a soul then Coleridge would
Read all man's runes of moral worth to find
Words to ease his fulminating mind,
Unrooted by torment while seeking the good.
He button-holes John Keats on Highgate Hill,
His subject nightingales and Pindaric odes
Which shrink away from pain's and sorrow's loads.
Beauty's essential joy confronts the ill!

Keats, on borrowed time, shy before the sage,
Finds in the torrent a firm rock to hold,
And climbs to find a view more clear and bold
Of beauty living beyond his human cage.
STC shook the hand of death and grief
And reached the chemist for opiate relief.

Wordsworth's birthday –
7th April 1770

Two hundred and fifty years since from the womb
A babe becomes a sleep, a dreaming star,
Seeking his soul to speak his spirit far
From clouds of glory in his earthly tomb.
The child finds Heaven in God, his natural home.
He fights the prison-house of memory lost.
His marching feet prints beauty in the frost.
Tenacious, he chants his vision as he roams
Thousands of miles of mountains, caverns, brooks.
The meanest flower, each new-born hopeful day
Keep careful watch over his mortality.
He captures innocent brightness in his books.
This baby's journey from light to celestial light
Speaks the soul's immensity and transcends night.

Mary Shelley reads Charlotte Turner Smith's sonnet and thinks of her Mother, Mary Woolstonecraft

So a wild man stood on a headland's peak.
Alone he stared at the monstrous sea
As its vital force raged like me
When my children died and I made a freak
From a lightning strike. From Spezia's maw
My husband sailed to die with friend and crew.
He dared to go where only dead men flew.
I suffered while he challenged nature's law.

You claim the conscious heart beats beyond a death.
Miscarriage's inherited blood is now my birth.
Mine is his heart from the ashes of mirth
Preserved in this casket, all that's left.
Mother, I was your child and a woman now.
I will write my future. You showed me how.

Stained Glass

Not what it seems when sight is refracted
In lozenges of glass in high windows blown
Through leaded diamonds neatly connected
To make a cracked image of God enthroned.
Turn from the mottled light as from a mirror
And, on grey stone, cloud-shadows chase blind
Fugitives seeking a rescue from terror.
While ruby light leaks tears of blood on lined
Granite walls, in this twilight blinded place,
Like Plato, I peer unseeing and darkly
Seeking compassion in each blank-eyed face.
Deflected rays through murdered saints only
Reflect a broken vision of pain and night.
Outside, the sunset bathes the sea with light.

Finding Shelley

His face is unfleshed and eyes are sockets.
Strings halo his puce crown like bleached seaweed.
Black velvet jacket and boyish breeches
Are stained with salt. Here, in this pocket,
A hastily folded book, another here.
Keats and Socrates were his companions
Before he dared the storm once too often.

Identify him from this evidence?
His flotsam resting place is concordant
With currents from Spezia gulf. Besides,
At other unsurprising locations,
There are his two fellow travellers
Thrown to the chasm by rashness,
Anger at rejection or, be honest,
Refusal ever to trim the sails.

Was Edward Williams the flying fool
Desperate to sail back to his woman?
Or Shelley seeking Utopia on speed
Through intermingling of soul with soul:
A chat-up line from poet to a girl?
There's no jealous competition for love
When Jane plucks music from her two-stringed
Guitar and soothes both temples with her touch.

He is matter now as red clay is matter,
Infinitely vacant, inanimate.
Beyond the pulsing particles of nothing,
Penned in the present eternity of death,
Refusing resurrection of the body,
What has he found? Incandescent flame
And the final cooling of his bubbling brain.

Summer Solstice in Spenserian Stanzas

With admiration for John Donne

It is the year's high noon and it is the day's
When zenith reached, the blaze of white-hot sun,
With scorching heat, aims its fiery gun
To scour the green to desert with laser rays.
The rolling sphere is poised
Between the chaos of unfolding doom, the noise
Of breaking seasons, discarded plastic toys.
It shines for truth or lie.
Decide to live with light or die.

Consider me then, you, claiming to be free
In the next world, the next year's embrace,
For I am a moth of dust, a mere trace
Of the hope and faith which once embodied me.
For this solstice sun burns
Away the very spirit that learns
Compassion from pain. This sun discerns
No shadow, and it is razored steel
Cutting and cauterising all that I feel.

Survive? I gaze on light and am blind
To past, present, future where my living dies.
I, by this blazing, am a zombie fried
Of all, that's nothing, in humankind.
Weep? My volcanic eyes spit blood
To drown the whole world, a flood
To bury carcasses in mud –
Forgotten souls, forgetting how to love
Self and other, refusing the dove.

But this dawning, with a mist upon the hill
And dew glistening on a spider's trap,
A red admiral spread its wings in the lap
Of a wide leaf, waiting to fulfil
Its destined day's need
For a mate to share its seed
For the sun to bring love and freed
Beauty in nectar-driven wavy flight.
It chose this day to ward off endless night.

So sun, balancing year to year,
Forgive and let your wonted beams
Remain a warming warning of what seems
An impossibility, a trembling fear
Of Earth's man-made destruction.
Gentle us with fresh love. Give instruction
To create, make invention.
Burned to the essence of nature's form,
Your light will renew, this creature reform.

Note on Thinkers and Poets

A friend shared a wonderful Cartier Bresson photograph of Jean Paul Sartre. He stands on Pont des Arts in Paris shortly after the end of the Second World War. I was inspired to write a sonnet from this picture, my thoughts about the time and Sartre's ideas about existence. This sonnet was fortunate enough to win the International Sonnet Competition mounted annually by the superb Better than Starbucks *poetry organisation in America. It was published in February 2022 in that journal.*

Meanwhile I was seeking photographs and articles about other philosophers in whom I had an interest, but this research spilled over into poets and writers I was reading both for their writing and for their philosophical reach. I have a particular interest in the Romantic Movement as a member of the Friends of Coleridge, hence STC with Keats in Highgate and Wordsworth's birthday joined the canon. The seven and eight line stanzas about Shelley's death follow no set rhyme pattern, but half rhymes and assonance abound. This, in turn, widened to a few more poets, more sonnets and one poem in Spenserian stanzas, but following Donne's pattern for his Nocturnal upon St Lucy's Day. *Iris Murdoch, Mary Shelley, Gertrude Turner Smith are female representatives in this list, the first because of her novels and work on metaphysics, Mary Shelley and Gertrude Smith for their Gothic writing.*

An earlier version of Auden and the Ashes of Anxiety *was published by* Better than Starbucks *in August 2022.*

POLEMICS

Psoriasis

Psoriasis scabs my fretful unleaved trees.
Roots writhe but fail to thrive in soil's lost health.
Fat corporations frack for fossil's wealth,
Build plastic island wastes in anxious seas.
Here sunsets crest the waves to make them bleed.
My carbon star won't heal a virus touch.
I fire out blanks, Monsanto on a crutch.
No longer can my growth beget a seed.

What cream or salve do war-rich men employ
when lightning pock-marks flesh with nuclear grit
to cheat perceptions with a fraudulent ploy?
They sell replacement bombs which are not fit
for immortal tales. But Earth will win release
By purging man to find a healing peace.

Parasite

Within this body lurks a parasite
knotting intestines in a greasy rope.
Unwelcome lodger saps a host to cope
with illness just this side of ruinous night.
It feeds off solid flesh with scarce a stain.
But fearful man sinks poison fangs in faults
and tears apart a planet. Now we're caught
by Earth's strong power in dark volcanic rain.

The Earth's not dying. It casts us off. We
ache for travel on another voyage
where a wealthy virgin offers rocket passage,
a space adventure where we may be free.
But cash presents no exit door to freedom.
It barricades the poor inside a fiefdom.

Blind Clarity

War spits its venom. Cobra chooses sides
With true conviction that the truth prevails
In victory over others' foolish prides.
Such certainty blind clarity unveils
And shames our wary and agnostic flight.
On the high hill of scepticism's doubt
We flaunt our flags. They fly in brazen light
And put our darker thoughts into a rout.

But certainty stalks life beyond our sight,
Deals casually in death being without
Passions or faith. It holds an army ready
For brutal combat called in blinkered night.
The bombs and bullets shot as lies on lies
Kill more than flesh when rightful honour dies.

National Saint

With numerous spondees and anapaests denying the iambic form.

By George, in Turkey, Syria, Bulgaria
This knight struts as a national saint!
Their red crosses on white are no rarer
Than forget-me-nots in gardens quaint
Set in warm dreamy Cotswold villages,
Or along the banks of Surrey's Thames
Hazy under clouds of biting midges,
Or where the backbone Pennines lines and hems
Stitched red and white roses on either side.
From Norfolk to Cornwall they shine their blue
Eyes winking at our hubristic snide
Insulation. We must learn to rue
The arrogance of ignoring all the rest
In the assumption that we own the vest!

Behind the Mask

Haiku

Mask behind mask
Goggle eyes behind goggles
I breathe in his fear

Insert essential
Oxygen to pump wet lungs
He inhales exhales

With gasping for life
The whole unit is heaving
Drowning on dry land

Watchet tide is high
It slicks up the river wall.
Moon shines on treacle.

Fifteen hour shift done
Alone I lie in my bed
The waves sigh and moan

Merman and mermaid
Seaweed-sequinned messengers
Bring tales of rebirth

Coda to Behind the Mask

Mask behind mask, goggle eyes behind goggles, I breathe in his fear. "Calm. Keep breathing." I insert oxygen to pump his wet lungs. He inhales, exhales; each gasp drowns him on dry land. I sweat in a plastic shroud. He had been a fisherman of carp, always returned his gaping prey to the lake.

"A stranded whale suffocates under its own weight," I whisper as his wheezing reaches out for its end. Waves heave and retreat, sigh and moan. I become his seaweed-sequinned mermaid moving to the off-switch. "Slip into the waters now and swim to the stars."

Rhyming Couplets for a Press Briefing

I will keep this briefing brief.
Spot my tissue not a spotted handkerchief.
Crocodile tears are what I shed
For the unnamed uncounted dead.
My shares in private medicine
Are protected. It would be a parlous sin
Not to extend my reach into profit
Through using my interest in protective kit
To corner the market. But look on the bright side,
Can't you? Crimes committed continue to slide.
The greens are applauding our cleaner air
While HS2 ploughs through trees. We don't care
About ancient woodlands or worker distances.
Protestors are at fault: too many instances
Of people breaking lock-down rules.
Stay safe in your cells and don't be fools.
Our beloved leader shows the proper way
Holed up in Chequers for another holiday,
A honeymoon or fortnight in the sun.
After glad-handing nurses, he had to run
To catch the bug, but he is a hero
To survive. Give it up for this zero-
Rated philanderer still living
While the old and their carers are giving
Themselves up for medical research.
Their corpses are antibodies. We lurch
From incompetence to blatant lies.
Just do as you're told. Clapping flies

On Thursdays cheers the NHS, stops the bug.
You'll feel much better as you lug
Your neighbours' shopping up the empty hill
Because your headache just needs a rapid pill.
I've shares in paracetemol of course
And an off-shore tax haven – unfair to force
Me to pay tax when charity's such fun,
As is obedience to Mr Murdoch's Sun.
Now drink your Dettol neat and shove your lamp
Up your anus. That's the treatment to stamp
Out disease. Are Trump's snake oil cons better
Than hypocrisy from an Eton liar?

Do Not Return

Do not return to what was once the normal
The Sun now casts an unpolluted ray.
If normal ruins lives, I'll be abnormal.

I wore a pin-stripe suit to be quite formal.
Pyjamas by a screen now start my day.
Do not return to what was once the normal.

Obscene wealth and rip-offs were the normal.
True workers need their true worth's monthly pay.
If normal ruins lives, I'll be abnormal.

Elitism made callousness the normal.
Doctors and nurses suffer in the bay.
Do not return to what was once the normal.

Johnson conjures lies to make them normal.
Divide and rule is still the fascist way.
If normal ruins lives, I'll be abnormal.

Hacking ancient woodlands was the normal
And fracking for more oil the sordid play.
Do not return to what was once the normal.
If normal ruins lives, I'll be abnormal.

Note on Polemical Poems

Polemical pieces so often become out-dated by new times and new circumstances, but the underlying anger builds when repeated scandals and disastrous leadership become rooted in a society. The great satirists of the eighteenth century spread their messages through the coffee and tea houses of London and hastily assembled posters and flyers. Now we have stand-up comedians, social media networks, radio and television. Newspapers owned by a few very rich people still have a circulation and influence. The verses in the Polemic section of this book are more varied in form than the sonnet. The impact of climate change and the blind autocratic nature of the power-brokers' response to it deserve more than my first three sonnets, but finding metaphors within a tortured framework managed to keep me relatively sane in the writing of them. Blind Clarity *has nothing new to say about war and lies which Auden didn't say far better, but I needed to include my take on this appalling abuse of power across the world.*

Behind the Mask *is a series of haikus and stemmed from talking with a nurse at a distance. She was coming off duty on a rainy night and had just staggered out of her car. It was eleven o'clock. She had served a straight fifteen hours and was exhausted, but due back early the next day. I scribbled the coda on my return from walking the dog and then created the haikus. Her face haunts me still.*

Do Not Return *is a villanelle. I fear it articulates a futile hope.*

NATURE

No Cage

The daily rut, the routine walk,
The staple diet of tea, no talk,
A little snooze, a flickering screen,
Each moment marked by where I've been
With dog, with bags, up hill, down town,
The passing wave, the smile, the frown,
Four beats per line, divided time
In tiny ripples to break the sign
That every day has now become
A common pattern, the total sum
Of being closed inside a box
Without a chisel to prize its locks.

But look, a sudden pulse, a shining skein
Weaving and sliding in the lane:
Three slow-worms young and freshly grown
Twine sinuous beauty round a stone.
And then a brimstone jerks and settles,
Wings of butter on spinach nettles.
No peregrine falcon steepling today
But a budgerigar has escaped to play
Along a sunlit branch. It does not stay
For my crumb. A strut, a nod, then gone.
"No cage for me!" It chirps its song.

Dawn-Fox

I started to write this sonnet with Ted Hughes's magnificent "Thought Fox" and "Horses" in mind. I felt inhibited by Hughes's imagery and power, but needed to try!

Midnight then first light for stone-still horses.
Dawn-fox brings new blessings and old curses.
I catch him flowing on dew-touched tip-toes.
Furnace-sculpted bronze freezes. One paw lifts
In benediction, for well he knows
Warrens of prey incubate prayerful gifts:
Mist-hidden rabbits in a sliver of sun.
He points brush to nose, inching motion,
Indistinct shadow of a triggered gun
Of intention. Killer, no emotion.
Eternity of now awaits explosion.
An unheard noise. He leaps, whirls to stand,
Eyes blazing, cursing food lost and his foe.
He flies over the cliff-edge where I won't go.

Garden Voice

Slowly miniscule moments of life's drab
Presence wince into being like a plant
Tempted into bud by the routine chant
Of a blackbird before it starts to stab
An earthworm. My pup launches with a crash
Across the dawn garden, then swerves to chart
His patch with tail erect, pretends to smart
At the bird's intrusion or wishes to play, to thrash
The undergrowth and nose out nests of plush
Lining where her dowdy young, yet to wing,
Cowering in their hiding, cannot sing
Their danger. But then a speckled thrush,
Purposeful, unfazed, shrub-shielded, sings.
Hushed, my dog returns and the garden rings.

Small Grave

The channel stays calm and the highest tide
Laps the cliffs with a repeated caress.
Shifting mist below the wide castle-ride
Masks this early morning's drifting loneliness.
Without you, passion becomes thin and wan.
Milky light shrouds Warren Bay's tangled trees.
I walk the routine uphill paths where gone
Are markers to the cliff-top's narrow frieze.

The green ledge edges sea and sky with blue.
Here lies a fledgling hunched inside a clump
Of fern. Pearls bead its baldness. It grew
Just so far and then upheaval and the slump
To this small grave. Through broken limbs of trees
The sun bursts through and finds me on my knees.

Treason

Blast! Snow-broken branches of the willow
Cast early seed-time fledglings to the mud
Where bald, sinewy, grey and drained of blood
They lie like shrivelled men upon a pillow.
I do not know what they might have become,
Warbler, tit, gold-crest, blackbird or sparrow,
All potential stripped to the bone and marrow
And left to freeze, their gaping beaks quite dumb.

A tabby cat stalks past – no interest
Shown, being intent on so much plumper fare.
Even a small observance? No, she does not care.
Her bowl is full indoors beside her nest.
Blizzards rage through man's disrupted seasons
And threaten daily life with sudden treasons.

Quest

"A terrible beauty is born" or so spoke Yeats
Imagining creation like a glorious beast
Bringing death and life in equal measure
Both holding beauty as the only treasure.
Strip off the blinkers from routine living.
Break the barricades. Invite invasion.
Seek the first cause, the deep occasion
Which startled us into taking and giving
Love and hate.
                    Ah but where is our trust
That this power transcends our body's needs,
That the universe balances death with seeds
Of new beginnings after the old rust?
Undefiled, comes creation, not mild but wild
With longing and loving, a questing child.

Truce

I don't deal in absolutes of good and evil.
Extremes are the products of emotion and ego,
Cliches like grist from a grinding mill.
I feel the tension of frost on deep snow.
I hear ragged rooks caw up to the hill
Where frozen branches of beeches wait
For hierarchical quarrels to finally still
Into cloud-shrouded night when hushed is the state.

Morning brings a gale that violently flings
Drifts over hedges. Mine is determined plodding
Over steep Western Hill. Sleet whisks and stings
My red-chapped face and inside my wadding
The battle of hot and cold is waging.
I call a truce. My body is ageing.

Easter Bonnet

Dawn brings sweet singing for this sonnet.
It pinks the pale beauty of a primrose
And silvers the river where it flows
Down to the estuary, and in this minute
It switches from promise to fulfilment
With bursting fresh sunlight on the crest
Of the old fort. Let darkness dreams fade and rest
For the planet turns and rings in merriment.

Pluck sudden beauty from a month of pain
Find joyous time to share life's glory
Bring renewal's solace to the eternal story
Of seeming loss and reach for truth again.
And so I deck with flowers a springtime bonnet
To celebrate with love a happy sonnet.

Precious

These slender wisps of green among the grey
Are hardly spotted from ten yards away
And yet I know that frost itself will stay
Its killing clutch on the promise of May.
January breaks ranks and blasts the alleyway
With tiger roars. Gale lashes hail to flay
Old plants into ribbons, back into clay
Into the old compost of yesterday.

Fear not, old man, Winter's frantic needling.
Its sting protects the future with its power
And deadens pain so that another flower
May find a root-hold, a precious seedling
Pushing above the fruitful earth to play
With Spring-time light and laughter this new day.

Wimbleball Lake

Two dogs and I walk round the morning lake.
Mist frizzles leaves and now the freckled
Water glistens below us where we take
Our course between green banks mottled
By sun and shade. Such calm is here I may
Forget the squalor of human decay
Where corruption has become the way
Of living and power a tawdry play.

Cyndyllan on his tractor broke the vow
Of communion with Nature's sweet approach.
Now jet planes blast the sky. The dogs cower
Before stillness returns in hushed reproach.
A child laughs at the falling of a tower
And plucks the velvet petals from a flower.
But full-grown people fear and feel no joy
When puerile monsters make the Earth their toy.

Cyndyllan on his Tractor, by the Welsh poet R.S. Thomas

Barn

Behind a moat of bleached hay
A ladder leads to wisps and loft-dust.
In the corner, one coke bottle – shared;
A single sandal – where is the other?
Across the back wall in chalk,
Now smudged, unclear,
Your funny fond words for me alone.

Through the slats I view the yard,
The gates, the field, the sea beyond
And, stretching out my fingers,
I can touch the broken waves
Where we swam. Ah there you are,
And I will wait. You know where I am.

For a Wedding

When speaking of love's vivid sunshine flowers
Do not forget the anxious hours and hesitations,
Gentle reassurances – fragile hopes in new seeds.

There is soft rain on sun-warmed leaves.
The dark earth feeds its richness into growth.
Feel its quiet strength deep in your roots
Building love upon love into sweetest fruits.

The moon rises and you yearn to hold each other.
But a sudden pulse of uncertainty
In the westerly breeze may touch you still.

Pause. Listen to the other's heart.
It is more precious than your own,
And in giving yours, all fears have flown.
Love fuses heart to heart as one
And charges moon and stars to shine as sun.

Myopia

Five pebbles, glistening with quartz,
each with different geometries
from different geologies,
crown a shelf of salt-frosted granite.

Read the runes: hieroglyphs scratched into stone
create a ballerina in white tutu etched on grey,
left leg poised in air, torso lifted,
still as Keats's man-made urn.

Discoveries: a stropped razor of flint,
bronze serrations on its edge;
a small di with one warped maroon side,
a cube, almost, and the *almost* seems Art;
pebble smooth as a lover's dimple.

Precise delineation: a circle compass-crisp,
flow of light streaming in bright lines
as if a breath could bubble-blow it away.
Yet aeons of fret and friction moulded this.

Persephone

She sits in her morning sun-trap
Silk scarf loose round her neck
While shaded eyes coolly check
The willow basket in her lap.
It is full of flowers beaded with dew.

She knows the rhythms –
Seed to earth to growth
And how the red soil harbours
Its power and then pulses
Pale shoots into glory
Almost in a winking of an eye.

And quick she is to spot
The precise combination
Of colour and shape within
A shadow-filled corner
To give it confidence,
Or how that crowded wall
Shelters shrubs better
After hard pruning.

She knows the fleeting magic
Of a wind-blown rose,
The unassuming pastels
Of a winged fritillary,
The almost black of a late tulip
Opening its velvet to summer heat.

Oh and these pyramids of green
Are topped with heavy-headed peonies
Like ruffled feather dusters
With the sun haloing them.

Blood-rimmed twilight spears
Are about to split their points
Into delicately veined geraniums
While swallows waltz towards heaven.

Here is Persephone scenting
Paths of thyme with soft tread.
Her evening approach lives
In the heady perfume of night stock
And honeysuckle sweetness.

We knew she was coming.
But not how, when or why now
With the fading of a bloom in Winter
Before the new cream of primrose.

But, as darkness falls and Hades demands
Her inexorable return,
Watch her strong spirit float away –
White lace reaching for the snowball tree,
Nurturing Spring life with Persephone.

Moorland Walk

Thinking of John Clare

Come, my adult children, come with me
Over the high moors clean and free.
Let us duck beside boulder and scree
To find small violets or late bilberry
Caught in rich peat gathered in the lee
Of the prevailing wind. On our approach
The grouse will chuck a guttural reproach
And chur away. Walk on to the next crest
Where the sky is nearer heaven and blessed
By a cairn stacked with tributary stones.
Last year's gorse is blackened finger-bones.

There! Another early grouse, we've counted seven
In just a hundred strides between the crags
Where bunched reeds spike and marshland sags
Beneath our boots like sodden rags.
The dog slides, belly-down, shakes and brags,
He scents the air and then, nose down, drags
Behind. In the high ground there's a gleam
Like frosted glass. Sun tricks each stone to seem
White diamonds or luscious cream
Before mist descends, cutting off the beam
With rain to make a dishcloth shroud.
Is it monstrous headland or swollen cloud?

Fear not, my children, every walk betrays
Moments of loss, remembrance of old ways. See
The sodden sheep know more than we
And continue on their scarcely spotted track
Around the point. Here there is no lack
Of shelter and the squall clears a crack.
Sunshine floods the gorse. It has the knack
Of catching each sprig of wool like tag,
Turning a rabbit scut to surrender flag.

Slide down where we found the devil's toenail
And careful over the rough-cut bridge. Don't fail
To swing right where Howden Moors show no trail.
Our route is round to Langsett where the stagecoach mail
Once reached the Waggon and Horses – a tacking sail
Over the ocean of moors. The grass is pale
Where Flouch waters ease to the weir
Where a chill breeze crosses the dam, but a mere
Mile reaches the inn. We'll eat beside the fire
And mention important things like larks, a jay, a choir
Of geese in skeins, their formation strung on wire,
And how great pairs of swans migrate so far
From Siberian depths, following a lodestar.

Pantoum of Deceit

Blackbirds trail their broken wings.
Deceit protects the unfledged young.
Their voice triumphant rings
When he who hides sticks out his tongue.

Deceit protects the unfledged young
But wary is the one who trusts
When he who hides sticks out his tongue
Sucks out the crumbs and leaves the crusts.

Deceit protects the unfledged young
When he who hides sticks out his tongue
But wary is the one who trusts
Sucks out the crumbs and leaves the crusts.

When he who hides sticks out his tongue
And grins his gall in blatant lies
Sucks out the crumbs and leaves the crusts
When he who hides sticks out his tongue.

Deceit protects the unfledged young
Their voice triumphant rings
When he who hides sticks out his tongue
Blackbirds trail their broken wings.

Solstice Spring Garden at Dawn

It is all light
all blue light and wind
all light blue and wind and sun.
Pink-veined satin-sheened heads
nod and strain to fly
in a whirling bright sky:
first magnolia buds
in solstice morning
of gust and gorgeous green.

It is all light
all primary light and wind
all first light and wind and sun
flash a scarlet arrow on cream
hug bleached sapling bark
showing maroon buds
to an emerald woodpecker
silvered as the smiling grass.
It seeks jewelled bugs in branches.

It is all light
all light quenched with shade then sun
all light chasing silver into mist.
Blood crown glistens and is matt,
but blackbird beaks sing gold.
Woodpecker launches and flies
into cuckoo egg blue.
Tail undulates like a magic carpet
Waving farewell and farewell and adieu.

Note on Nature Poems

Most of these poems were written during strict lockdown and are immediate to that time, but I have included some that were re-awakened through this period and revisited as memories of place and people. Barn *was one of the successful poems in the Guernsey poetry competition of 2021.* To a Wedding *was read by a friend at his daughter's wedding.* Persephone *was part of the celebration of the life of a dear friend.* Moorland Walk *harks back to a shared walk with my adult children. Gradually my poems have become more instinctive and free again, but the use of rhyme, half rhyme, enriching assonance, occasional regularly stressed line, repetition for effect are incorporated and celebrated, at least by me!*

These poems serve to reassure me that love holds us together in how we share and appreciate this beautiful planet in our brief and potentially glorious lives. The Pantoum speaks of how all creatures find ways of survival and sacrifice for the continuation of life. The trailing blackbird's wing is just one example. What are our ways through which we can survive and prosper? Auden suggests in one of his sonnets that an idea outlives death. I would argue that without ideas for renewal and the application of them through compassion and kindness, we are already dead. The final Spring Solstice poem sings of such freshness and potential for renewal. Fortunately, the spirit of creation and cooperation continues to burn and will lead us away from the malaise of greed and destruction.

Acknowledgements

My gratitude to David Fairer and Kate Innes for their reading of an early draft and their helpful responses to it. Thank you to Ben Johnson for his portrait photograph of me – far more than a "mug-shot"! Thank you to the whole Troubador team guiding this book into publication and, in particular, Beth Archer for her careful and efficient support and Raisa Patel for her clarity about marketing and publicity. Thanks too to Adrian and Anna Eden at "By the Book" for their encouragement and to Paul Berry, whose fine poetry collection "Towards Babingley", published through Troubador, convinced me that "Forms from Chaos" would be in good hands. Some of these poems have been shared with friends at Chalk River Poets, Fakenham. I greatly value their supportive and constructive suggestions. Thank you to Carol Ann Duffy for granting permission to include an excerpt from her sonnet, "Prayer".

About the Author

A graduate of Trinity College, Oxford, Ian Enters worked in Education and became Adviser for English and the Arts in Sheffield. He is a published author of four collections of poetry, four novels and libretti for school/community musicals. He wrote and produced the opera "Avalon". Most recent publication: "Word Hoard", translations and re-workings of Anglo-Saxon and medieval poetry.